BLUE BANNER
BIOGRAPHY

J.J.
WATT

Cliff Mills

Mitchell Lane
PUBLISHERS

P.O. Box 196
Hockessin, Delaware 19707
Visit us on the web: www.mitchelllane.com

Mitchell Lane
PUBLISHERS

Printing   1   2   3   4   5   6   7   8   9

Blue Banner Biographies

5 Seconds of Summer	Ice Cube	Miguel Tejada
Abby Wambach	Ja Rule	Mike Trout
Adele	Jamie Foxx	Nancy Pelosi
Alicia Keys	Jason Derulo	Natasha Bedingfield
Allen Iverson	Jay-Z	Nicki Minaj
Ashanti	Jennifer Hudson	One Direction
Ashlee Simpson	Jennifer Lopez	Orianthi
Ashton Kutcher	Jessica Simpson	Orlando Bloom
Avril Lavigne	J.J. Watt	P. Diddy
Blake Lively	J. K. Rowling	Peyton Manning
Blake Shelton	Joe Flacco	Pharrell Williams
Bow Wow	John Legend	Pink
Brett Favre	Justin Berfield	Pit Bull
Britney Spears	Justin Timberlake	Prince William
Bruno Mars	Kanye West	Queen Latifah
CC Sabathia	Kate Hudson	Rihanna
Carrie Underwood	Katy Perry	Robert Downey Jr.
Chris Brown	Keith Urban	Robert Pattinson
Chris Daughtry	Kelly Clarkson	Ron Howard
Christina Aguilera	Kenny Chesney	Russell Wilson
Ciara	Ke$ha	Sean Kingston
Clay Aiken	Kevin Durant	Selena
Cole Hamels	Kristen Stewart	Shakira
Condoleezza Rice	Lady Gaga	Shia LaBeouf
Corbin Bleu	Lance Armstrong	Shontelle Layne
Daniel Radcliffe	Leona Lewis	Soulja Boy Tell 'Em
David Ortiz	Lil Wayne	Stephenie Meyer
David Wright	Lionel Messi	Taylor Swift
Derek Jeter	Lindsay Lohan	T.I.
Drew Brees	LL Cool J	Timbaland
Dwyane Wade	Ludacris	Tim McGraw
Eminem	Luke Bryan	Tim Tebow
Eve	Mariah Carey	Toby Keith
Fergie	Mario	Usher
Flo Rida	Mary J. Blige	Vanessa Anne Hudgens
Gwen Stefani	Mary-Kate and Ashley Olsen	Will.i.am
Hope Solo	Megan Fox	Zac Efron

Library of Congress Cataloging-in-Publication Data
Mills, Cliff, 1947–
J.J. Watt / by Cliff Mills.
       pages cm. — (Blue Banner Biographies)
Includes index.
Audience: Age: 5-9.
Audience: Grade: K to Grade 3.
ISBN 978-1-68020-085-0 (library bound)
1. Watt, J.J., 1989– —Juvenile literature. 2. Football players—United States—Biography—Juvenile literature. I. Title.
GV939.W362M55 2015
796.332092—dc23
[B]
                                                                                          2015003205
eBook ISBN: 978-1-68020-086-7

ABOUT THE AUTHOR: Cliff Mills has written many biographies of world leaders, sports superstars, and entertainment stars. He is a Carter-Woodson Award Honorable Mention from the National Council for Social Studies. He has followed J.J. Watt's career from its earliest days at the University of Wisconsin, and roots against him only when the Texans play the New England Patriots. Mills lives in Jacksonville, Florida with his wife Rosemary and his football memorabilia.

PUBLISHER'S NOTE: The following story has been thoroughly researched and to the best of our knowledge represents a true story. While every possible effort has been made to ensure accuracy, the publisher will not assume liability for damages caused by inaccuracies in the data and makes no warranty on the accuracy of the information contained herein. This story has not been authorized or endorsed by J.J. Watt.

Blue Banner Biography

Watt proudly wears and carries red, white, and blue for a game against the Cincinnati Bengals at NRG Stadium in Houston, Texas.

The Legend Begins

On a bright and sunny Saturday afternoon January 7, 2012, thousands of excited fans began arriving at Reliant Stadium in Houston, Texas. Some had red and blue face paint with strings of beads and wigs to match. They were there to watch the most important game the Houston Texans had ever played. It was a National Football League (NFL) playoff game against the Cincinnati Bengals. The winner would move on into the next round of the playoffs and the loser would go home. The Houston Texans had never won a playoff game.

At the kickoff, more than 71,000 fans rose to their feet. The roar was deafening. But it was the Bengals and their quarterback, Andy Dalton, who started strong. They outplayed the Texans for most of the first half of the game. Late in the second quarter, the Bengals had the ball on their 33-yard line. Dalton received the hike from his center and began looking up the field. He got ready to throw a pass to his sensational rookie receiver, A.J. Green. One of the Texans' defensive linemen, number 99, pushed his blocker backward toward Dalton. The defender kept his eyes on the

Bengals' quarterback, to his right. He watched Dalton's eyes and hands and how far back he had stepped.

Number 99, J.J. Watt was tall at six feet five inches (195.6 cm) and strong. But he was also fast and quick thinking. As Dalton started to throw, the Texans' defender knew he was too late to sack (tackle for a loss) the quarterback. So, instead, he jumped into the way of the pass. He timed his jump perfectly. The football travelled only a few yards. But instead of batting it down, the defender snatched the ball out of the air with both hands and intercepted the ball. Then, number 99 ran and no one could stop him. He would joke later that all he wanted to do was not fall down.

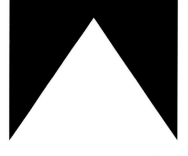

Number 99, J.J. Watt was tall at six feet five inches (195.6 cm) and strong. But he was also fast and quick thinking.

When he crossed the goal line, he put up both hands to signal, "Touchdown." He saluted the fans in the end zone, and then his teammates mobbed him. The Texans' fans celebrated, loudly rocking the stadium.

It was not only the play of the game; it was one of the biggest plays in the Houston Texans' football history. The legend of J.J. Watt, number 99, began that day.

The Bengals never scored after the interception. The Texans won, 31 to 10.

Watt told reporters after the game, "There's a lot of people who counted me out . . . People didn't believe in me and now to do something like that in an NFL playoff game, it's truly special."

J.J. celebrates sacks by saluting, to show his respect for the military and for fans.

Only three years earlier, Watt had dropped out of college. He had been delivering pizzas and mopping floors. Even though he had been a great player in high school, several big-college football coaches did not think he could play well enough to deserve a scholarship. He would prove them wrong.

J.J. Watt wears a wristband that says, "Dream Big. Work Hard." To get to that playoff moment, his big dreams came true because of his hard work in training and on the practice field. His dreams began in a small city in Wisconsin.

Watt is an old school and powerful player who can play both offense and defense, and trains for both.

Dreaming Big

Justin James (J.J.) Watt was born on March 22, 1989, in Pewaukee, Wisconsin. He grew up in Pewaukee, which was a small city of 13,000 people back in 2010. Located in southeastern Wisconsin, Pewaukee is about twenty miles from Milwaukee and just north of Waukesha. It is a beautiful place, with rolling green fields and forests that turn red and orange in the fall. Near its center is a clear, shimmering, blue lake.

J.J.'s mother is Connie Watt. She grew so big during J.J.'s pregnancy people thought she was having twins. After J.J. was born, Connie gave birth to two more sons: Derek who is three years younger than J.J, and T.J. two years younger than Derek. They too would grow up to be tall and play football.

Like many mothers, Connie played many roles. She had a career working for a building-inspection company, first as a secretary and then as vice-president. J.J. tweeted on Mother's Day 2014, "Thank you Mom for delicious meals, homework help, rides to practice, instilling discipline, unconditional love."

J.J.'s father is John Watt, who recently retired as a firefighter and emergency medical services worker for the Waukesha Fire Department. When J.J. was born, John was working 24-hour shifts. He would call home to have Connie put J.J. on the phone, to hear their baby laugh or cry, and that helped John get through the long hours.

Like many fathers, John played catch with his sons and they played football and baseball. John saw them off to school on many days, and he told them to "act like somebody."

Pewaukee's elementary, middle, and high schools are on the same campus. So J.J. was lucky enough to go to the same school before he entered college.

J.J.'s dreams started early. In fourth grade, he told teacher Judy Keefe, "I really want to be in the NFL." She told him he could do that if he worked hard. Watt told *Houston Chronicle* Tania Ganguli, "I learned quickly that people don't take dreams like that seriously." He was lucky to have a teacher who understood, a teacher who knew that a dream could become a goal.

J.J.'s back yard was really several back yards in a row, a field of dreams without too many trees. JJ could get his best friend Kyle, his brothers, and other neighborhood children to play football any time. J.J. told Ganguli, "It was awesome."

But J.J.'s first sports love was hockey. He learned to ice skate when he was three years old. He told Anthony Witrado of the *Milwaukee Journal Sentinel* that hockey "was my best sport by far. That's actually my true passion." As they grew, the three Watt boys could frequently be found playing hockey in the family basement.

But hockey became expensive, partly because J.J.'s feet grew so big by the time he was thirteen years old that he needed custom-made skates. So he turned to other sports.

Each sport taught him something that he would use later in his life as a superstar athlete.

J.J. played baseball, as a pitcher, catcher, and shortstop, and his reflexes got faster.

He played basketball in high school, and averaged thirteen points a game in his senior year. He was best at blocking shots and getting rebounds. He learned to jump high and time the jumps well.

He threw a shot put far enough his senior year in 2007 to break his father's school record at Pewaukee High School. He gained power in his upper body and he used that power to advantage in sports.

Watt told Witrado, "I definitely think multiple sports are the way to go, especially in high school . . . I'd never suggest playing just one sport." He continued, "Sports has taught me discipline, leadership skills, and work ethic, things that can apply outside of the playing field."

The Watts made sure their three sons worked hard, played hard, and ate well. The boys burned so many calories working out and practicing sports that dinner was served around 4:30 P.M. and then again around 8:00 P.M.

J.J. had a great senior season playing football for the Pewaukee High School Pirates. He was a better tight end (an offensive player who catches passes and blocks) than he was a defensive end (a player who tries to tackle running backs and quarterbacks). He was named first-team all state on offense and honorable mention on defense. He was named the *Milwaukee Journal Sentinel* "Male Athlete of the Year" in 2007. J.J. made his parents especially proud by becoming a National Honor Society member and a high school honor student.

J.J. was now ready to take his game to the next level. He was ready to play college football.

Watt was a key player in the University of Wisconsin's 48-28 victory over the University of Michigan on November 20, 2010 at Michigan Stadium in Ann Arbor, Michigan.

Working Hard

J.J. had dreamed of going to the University of Wisconsin. But his real growth spurt had come late. At roughly 228 pounds at the end of his high school senior year, he was too small to get a scholarship at Wisconsin. He told ESPN reporter Jeffri Chadiha, "the thing that hurt me most was that nobody got to see my work ethic up close and personal." So, he chose to go to a college that would give him a full scholarship, Central Michigan University.

When he enrolled in the fall of 2007, he became the starting tight end. But he caught only eight passes, and the coaches told him they wanted to move him to offensive tackle after the season. Connie told Chadiha, "You could see that he wasn't happy . . . It's just hard for J.J. to give something if his heart isn't completely into it."

He then made a big decision that changed his life. He left Central Michigan and his scholarship. He told his parents that he needed to borrow some money from them for a year's tuition at Wisconsin. He hated to ask. But he said he would prove to the coaches there that he deserved a scholarship. For now, he told his parents, he would live with them and get a job.

J.J. took a job delivering pizza and mopping floors for Pizza Hut in Pewaukee. One day he was delivering a pizza to a home and a little boy answered the door. The boy recognized the football star from Pewaukee High and asked his mother, "Why is J.J. Watt here?" He was confused. How could the football star not be in college? Watt told Jeffri Chadiha that he went back to his car, embarrassed. He hated that he had disappointed the boy who had looked up to him. He knew he needed to find a way to make that boy look up to him again. "I was learning a lot of things about myself by going through those times. I felt like I had so much that I wanted to show people and they just couldn't see it." He would make them see.

J.J. never gives up, even when he is on the ground. Here he is tackling New York Giants quarterback Eli Manning in a game at MetLife Stadium in September 2014.

During the winter and spring of 2008, J.J. trained as he had never trained before. He ate six meals a day. He ate a lot of vegetables and chicken, and drank protein shakes. He increased his time with Brad Arnett, a physical trainer who owned NX Level Sports in Waukesha. He lifted weights, flipped monster truck tires, and pushed heavy sleds. He pushed himself to his breaking point, and then he pushed more. He made himself bigger, faster, and stronger. He got better at getting better. A boy became a man.

By the time J.J. arrived at the University of Wisconsin in the summer of 2008, he weighed 270 pounds. He could bench press more than 400 pounds. Defensive coach Charlie Partridge noticed him and thought Watt could switch from offense to defense. J.J. made the practice squad as a defensive end, playing against regular players on offense.

Partridge let Watt watch game film in his office after dinner. J.J. told Elizabeth Merrill of *ESPN — The Magazine*, "If I ever got sick of it and thought, 'Man, I could be doing something else,' I'd look behind me at the stadium and picture myself on game day, making plays."

In the spring of 2009, J.J.'s hard work paid off. He was offered a scholarship. The first time Watt ran out of the tunnel for a game in Camp Randall Stadium (the Wisconsin Badgers' field), Connie broke down in tears. She told

> *J.J. trained as he had never trained before. He ate six meals a day. He ate a lot of vegetables and chicken, and drank protein shakes.*

reporter Ashley Schumacher, "I know how hard he worked for it, and how hard he trained for it."

In the next two years, J.J. proved himself. He began single-handedly to destroy offensive plays. Even though the offensive linemen knew what the play was, and he didn't, he reacted so quickly that he was usually in the right spot at the right time.

J.J. Watt was named to the All-Big Ten in 2010 and second-team All-American. He won the Lott Trophy in December 2010, given to the best defensive player in college football.

He was named to the All-Big Ten in 2010 and second-team All-American. He won the Lott Trophy in December 2010, given to the best defensive player in college football. That year he led the Wisconsin Badgers with 21 tackles for a loss and seven sacks. In his last regular season game at home the crowd began chanting his name after he made a late-game tackle. Watt told Ganguli, "This is everything you dream about as a kid." Of course, Connie's eyes filled with tears, just as they had before his first game.

J.J.'s last game as a Wisconsin Badger was the most painful. On January 1, 2011, Texas Christian University (TCU) beat Wisconsin in the Rose Bowl, held in Pasadena, California. The score was 21 to 19. The TCU quarterback was Andy Dalton.

Less than a week later, on January 6, 2011, J.J. announced that he would enter the NFL draft. He wanted to make another dream come true.

In his last game as a college player, Watt's Wisconsin Badgers lost to the Texas Christian University Horned Frogs at the 97th Rose Bowl in Pasadena, California on January 1, 2011.

Watt has great hands on offense as well, as he is shown catching a touchdown pass from Ryan Mallett against the Cleveland Browns on November 16, 2014 at FirstEnergy Stadium in Cleveland, Ohio.

Turning the Boos
to Cheers

*T*he 2011 NFL Draft was held at Radio City Music Hall in New York City. On the first day of the draft, April 28, Watt's name was called out as the number eleven pick, in the first round. He was going to the Houston Texans.

The draft was being shown on a large screen at Reliant Stadium, and the boos started. J.J. heard them, and they hurt.

One fan told reporter Tania Ganguli that he was cancelling his season tickets. Another said it was a wasted pick. Once again, some people just couldn't see what he could do. But one fan cheered. J.J. later said he would find that fan some day and thank him.

A few days later at a press conference in Houston, Texans' defensive coach Wade Phillips introduced J.J. He told reporters, including Elizabeth Merrill, "He's big, he's athletic, he's smart." He had gained twenty more pounds of muscle in college. He held up one of J.J.'s hands, and said they were the biggest hands of the players who had tried out at the NFL Combine a few months before. And soon YouTube watchers saw Watt jumping fifty-five inches

A big dream comes true for the whole family when J.J. is drafted by the Houston Texans on April 28, 2011 at Radio City Music Hall in New York.

straight up onto a box, from a standstill. That is an almost impossible feat for a man weighing close to two hundred ninety-five pounds.

Even before he started playing for the Texans, he made some special fans. ESPN's Rick Reilly reported on a friendship J.J. had made. On July 2, 2011, the Berry family was driving home from their family vacation in Lubbock, Texas. A distracted driver hit their car head-on. Mr. and Mrs. Berry were killed, and their three children were hurt. J.J. visited them in their hospital room thirteen days later. Aaron, one of the boys, told Reilly, "J.J. Watt came in. I was shocked. I couldn't take the smile off my face." J.J. made friends with all three children. He shoots hoops with them and he plays cards with them. An aunt and uncle are raising the Berry children. Their uncle Peter told Reilly, "I could tell

[Watt] just liked to give to other people . . . He teaches you to never give up."

J.J. told reporter Elizabeth Merrill, "You have to be a nice guy off the field . . . But as soon as you step onto the field, you have to turn into a monster."

J.J. went to work and proved the Texans right for drafting him. In his very first NFL game on September 11, 2011 at Reliant Stadium, the Texans beat the Indianapolis Colts, 34 to 7. J.J. led his team with five tackles, he recovered a fumble, and he helped lead his team to the playoffs.

But it was his 2012 season that showed that he could be a brute-force monster and a bone-crusher on the field. In one game against the New York Jets, on October 8, 2012, Jet quarterback Mark Sanchez went back to pass late in the

Watt always works hard, here winning a tough fight for the ball and recovering quarterback Andrew Luck's fumble in a game against the Colts on October 9, 2014.

game. His team was behind 23 to 17 and he wanted to throw the game-winning touchdown at home on Monday Night Football. He saw his receiver break open and he threw the pass. J.J. was being blocked but had been watching Sanchez. Watt spun away from his blocker at the last second, and knocked the pass down. Announcer Jon Gruden called him "J.J. Swatt." The game was over and the Texans had won.

On October 21, 2012, at Reliant Stadium, the Texans played the Baltimore Ravens. The Texans had never beaten the Ravens. The game was close in the second quarter when Raven quarterback Joe Flacco went back to pass. J.J. batted the pass into the hands of one of his teammates, who ran 52 yards for a touchdown. That gave the Texans a 16 to 3 lead. Flacco seemed to second-guess himself after that, and the Texans won 43 to 13.

Merrill wrote about both the monster and the nice guy after that game. J.J. led the league in sacks; pass deflections for linemen, and marriage proposals. Merrill noted that Watt goes to his favorite restaurant and stands in line for more than an hour because he doesn't want special treatment. He says, "I wasn't raised to be a big shot."

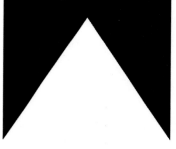

Merrill noted that Watt goes to his favorite restaurant and stands in line for more than an hour because he doesn't want special treatment. He says, "I wasn't raised to be a big shot."

J.J.'s 2012 season may be the best season any defensive player has ever had in the NFL. Gregg Rosenthal of NFL.com wrote that Watt had fifty-six "defeats." A defeat is a forced turnover, a tackle for a loss, or play that stopped a

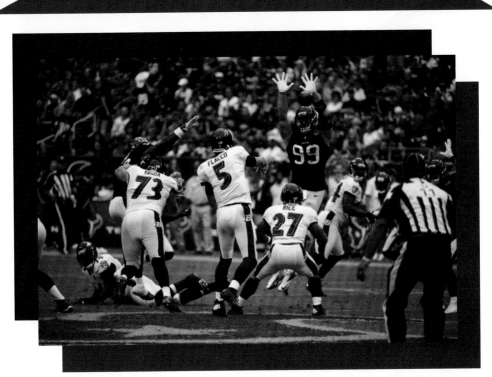

J.J. shows his quarterback-rattling "jazz hands" (waving with palms out, fingers spread) against the Ravens' Joe Flacco in a game at Reliant Stadium.

drive (either a tackle or deflected pass). The all-time high before J.J. was Ray Lewis's forty-five in 1999. J.J. had won many of the wars fought at the line of scrimmage. His speed, strength, and intelligence had taken away the advantage the offense had of knowing when the ball was going to be snapped and what was going to happen. He had kept his balance and made others lose theirs.

J.J. was named to the Pro Bowl (the NFL all-star game), and played well in it on January 27, 2013 in Aloha Stadium in Honolulu, Hawaii. He was then given the highest honor of all and named the AP NFL Defensive Player of the Year on February 2, 2013. Rosenthal wrote, "It would have been a crime if anyone else had won . . . It's hard to remember a player quite like Watt."

Colts quarterback Andrew Luck finds double trouble as he gets sacked high and low by Joe Mays and Watt during a game at Reliant Stadium in November 2013.

CHAPTER 5

A Time To Be Great

Christian Beasley has a rare blood disease that prevents him from going outside his home. His body can't fight germs well enough. So he goes to school at home, but has a robot to help. The robot goes to class and sends video and messages back to Christian's laptop computer. Christian named his robot "Watt" after one of his heroes.

NFL Films captured a visit to Christian's house in Splendora, Texas, in the spring of 2013. Christian was working on his math homework. J.J., wearing a red Texans jersey, came up behind him and said, "What's up buddy. I'm J.J. Nice to meet you, man." Christian was near tears with joy. His mother said that was a day he would never forget.

This is but one of the many acts of kindness J.J. is becoming famous for. While he was a junior in college, he formed the J.J. Watt Foundation, which donates money to after-school athletic programs in low-income areas in Wisconsin and Texas. Watt's tweets show just how generous he and the foundation are.

On the field, the 2013 season was one that the Houston Texans would like to forget. Injuries, quarterback changes, coaching changes, and more weakened the team. Their 2013 record was two wins and 14 losses. Watt still had a good year, with 80 tackles, ten-and-a-half sacks, and seven passes tipped or knocked down. But he was a bright light in a dark year.

Watt's fame skyrocketed in 2014. His commercials for Verizon have run constantly, showing how bad a dancer he can be. His face has been on magazine covers and billboards. In one cover story, *ESPN – The Magazine* writer Michael J. Mooney wrote that Watt rarely goes anywhere now without being mobbed by fans wanting a picture or an autograph. J.J. has adopted Texas and it has adopted him. He likes ranches and cowboy boots. He told Mooney, "I'll always be a Wisconsin boy at heart. But I'll always have sort of a connection with Texas."

Where there is fame, fortune often follows. J.J. signed a $100,000,000 contract in September 2014. He bought a car for his mother. He did a Google Internet search to see what rich people buy, and he was not impressed.

On the field, Watt is still a monster. He can line up at several positions, mostly left and right defensive end, but he can blitz from anywhere. He even lined up as a tight end on offense and caught three touchdowns in 2014 (on September 14, November 16, and November 30). On September 28, 2014, he intercepted a pass from Buffalo Bills' quarterback E.J. Manuel and returned in eighty yards for a touchdown. A week later he returned a fumble for a score against the Colts. He became one of only four defensive players in NFL history to catch a touchdown pass on offense, intercept a pass for a touchdown, and return a fumble for a score, all in the same season. J.J. Watt is also the first defensive player since 1944 to score at least five touchdowns in a season. On

November 30, 2014, the home crowd chanted "M-V-P" (Most Valuable Player) to their hero.

Watt has paid a price for his success. He told *Houstonia Magazine* writer Peter Holley, "I live my life dedicated to this game. I'm not married. I don't have kids. I sacrifice fun." He leaves his house in Pearland around 5:30 a.m. and is one of the first at the Texans' training facility. He is one of the last to leave, studying quarterbacks and their deliveries, and blockers. He told Mooney, "You only get so much time to be as great as you can be."

Sports Illustrated writer Peter King asked Watt what he would do when his pro football career was over. Watt said he would want to be a high school football coach. "Inside all of us football players, we love football. We want to coach it and be able to mold young kids into great people." He wants to use his fame for good. "I just love to . . . connect with fans and try to do one small thing to help their lives."

He told Ganguli that he wants to marry, build a log cabin on a hill overlooking Pewaukee Lake, and "live the simple life that he lived as a child." He and his family will have dogs and maybe some horses. They'll have a boat on the lake.

For his opponents, those days can't come soon enough. But for many more years, barring serious injury, Watt will continue to push his blockers around with a controlled fury. He will run over them and through them. He will terrorize quarterbacks, running them down and swatting away their passes when he doesn't catch them. The number 99 monster will haunt their dreams. But the great warriors can turn off their anger after the battle. This friendly giant will give back to his fans. He will inspire many of them to dream big and work hard.

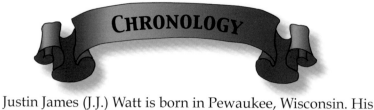

1989   Justin James (J.J.) Watt is born in Pewaukee, Wisconsin. His mother is Connie Watt and his father is John Watt.

2006   Watt is named First-Team All-Woodland Conference; he also is a National Honor Society member and on the Pewaukee High School High Honor Roll.

2007   Watt is named Male Athlete of the Year by the *Milwaukee Sentinel Journal*. He graduates from Pewaukee High School. He enrolls at Central Michigan University and plays tight end on offense.

2008   Watt leaves Central Michigan University and begins work at Pizza Hut in Pewaukee. He trains intensely during winter and spring and enrolls at the University of Wisconsin in the fall.

2009   Watt is granted a scholarship to play football at the University of Wisconsin. He plays in the fall as a defensive end. Watt majors in life sciences and communication.

2010   Watt plays defensive end for the University of Wisconsin and is a standout. He helps lead the team to the Rose Bowl. He is named to the All-Big Ten First Team and AP Second-Team All-American. In December, he is awarded the Lott Trophy, given to the best defensive player in college football.

2011   Watt plays in the Rose Bowl in Pasadena, California, on January 1. He announces he will be leaving Wisconsin for the NFL draft, and he is drafted by the Houston Texans in the first round on April 28. In his first regular season as a professional, he leads the team in tackles against the Colts on September 11.

2012   Watt has big games against the Jets on *Monday Night Football* on October 8 and against the Ravens on October 21. He is named to the Pro Bowl.

2013   On January 27, Watt plays in the Pro Bowl in Hawaii. He is named the AP NFL Defensive Player of the Year on February 2.

2014   Watt signs a one hundred million dollar contract in September. He becomes one of only four defensive players in NFL since 1944 to score at least five touchdowns in a single season. He is named AFC Defensive Player of the Week for week four.

2015   Watt recovered a fumble, had an interception, and swatted down three passes on the way to being named Defensive Most Valuable Player in the 2015 Pro Bowl, played in Glendale, Arizona, on January 25.

STATISTICS

Year	Team	Games Played	Tackles	Sacks	Fumbles Recovered	Passes Caught	Yards	TD
2011	Houston	16	48	5.5	2	0	0	0
2012	Houston	16	69	20.5	2	0	0	0
2013	Houston	16	65	10.5	2	0	0	0
2014	Houston	16	59	20.5	5	4	4	3
Career		64	241	57	11	4	4	3

AWARDS

2006 Woodland Conference (Wisconsin) Player of the Year.
All-Wisconsin player as both tight end and defensive end.
National Honor Society Member.
Pewaukee High School High Honor Roll.

2007 Athlete of the Year, *Milwaukee Journal Sentinel*.
Wisconsin State Champion, Shot Put.

2009 Honorable Mention, All-Big Ten.

2010 AP Second Team All-American.
First Team All-Big Ten.
Wisconsin Badgers Most Valuable Player.

2011 Houston Texan Rookie of the Year.
Pro Football Weekly All-Rookie Team.

2012 Houston Texans' Most Valuable Player.
AP Defensive Player of the Year.
AP First-Team All Pro.
AFC Defensive Player of the Week, for weeks two and fifteen.
AFC Defensive Player of the Month, September and December.

2013 First Team All-Pro Pro Bowl Selection.
Two blocked kicks, a Houston Texan record for one season.
Watt has thirty-six-and-a-half sacks in first three seasons, the seventh-most in NFL history for a player in his first three seasons.

2014 Pro Bowl Selection and Pro Bowl team captain.
First defensive player since 1944 to score five touchdowns in a season.

FURTHER READING

Books

Jacobs, Greg. *The Everything Kids' Football Book: All-time Greats, Legendary Teams, and Today's Favorite Players.* Seattle, Washington: Amazon Digital Services, 2014.

Works Consulted

Chadiha, Jeffri. "J.J. Watt Is Determined to Deliver." *ESPN.com*, April 7, 2011. http://sports.espn.go.com/nfl/draft2011/columns/story?id=6300367

Ganguli, Tanis. "The Life and Times of J.J. Watt." *The Houston Chronicle*, October 13, 2012. http://www.chron.com/sports/texans/article/The-life-and-times-of-J-J-Watt-3945755.php

Holley, Peter, and Justin Calhoun. "Watt's Inside: A Star Becomes a Superstar." *Houstonia Magazine*, August 1, 2013. http://www.houstoniamag.com/news-and-profiles/articles/watts-inside-august-2013

King, Peter. "The Monday Morning Quarterback: J.J. Watt, Supercharged." *Sports Illustrated.com*, September 4, 2013. http://mmqb.si.com/2013/09/04/jj-watt-unplugged/

Merrill, Elizabeth. "J.J. Watt — Mayberry and Mayhem." *ESPN – The Magazine*, November 12, 2012. http://espn.go.com/nfl/story/_/page/hotread-jjwatt/nfl-hot-read-houston-texans-jj-watt-seemingly-born-play-game

Mooney, Michael J. "Is J.J. Watt the Next Texas Legend?" *ESPN – The Magazine*, November 13, 2014. http://espn.go.com/nfl/story/_/id/11832806/can-jj-watt-become-texas-legend

NFL Films. "J.J. Watt's Inner Drive." *YouTube*, October 28, 2013. https://www.youtube.com/watch?v=5_uQW6y1DIs

Reilly, Rick. "J.J. Watt's Remarkable Friendship." *ESPN.com*, December 12, 2012. YouTube, https://www.youtube.com/watch?v=sSfkq7cXljo

Rosenthal, Gregg. "J.J. Watt Near Unanimous Defensive Player of the Year." *NFL.com*, February 2, 2013. http://www.nfl.com/news/story/0ap1000000134299/article/jj-watt-near-unanimous-defensive-player-of-the-year

Schumacher, Ashley. "My Three Sons: Badger Mom Proud of Watt Brothers On, Off the Field." *University of Wisconsin Alumni News*, August 24, 2014. http://www.uwalumni.com/news/badger-mom-connie-watt/

Solomon, Jerome. "Texans First-Round Pick Watt Driven to Succeed." *Houston Chronicle*, April 30, 2011. http://www.chron.com/sports/texans/article/Solomon-Texans-first-round-pick-Watt-driven-to-1685537.php

Spousta, Tom. "Texans Rookie Makes a Play as Big as His Dreams." *The New York Times*, January 10, 2012. http:www.nytimes.com/2012/01/11/sports/football/Texans-rookie-converts-doubters-with-big-plays.html

Tapper, Christina. "J.J. Watt Is Your Worst Nightmare." *Sports Illustrated Kids*, October 17, 2013. http://www.sikids.com/blogs/2013/10/17/jj-watt-is-your-worst-nightmare

Witrado, Anthony. "More Than One Field of Dreams: Pewaukee Senior a Multi-sport Standout." *Milwaukee Journal Sentinel*, June 17, 2007. http://www.jsonline.com/sports/preps/29374359.html

On the Internet

Houston Texans: "Player Roster and Information" http://www.houstontexans.com/team/roster/jj-watt/b44e970b-c671-a527-8ecc06f5b7b9/

J.J. Watt on Twitter https://mobile.twitter.com/JJWatt

Pro Football Reference.com "Career Statistics" http://www.pro-football-reference.com/players/W/WattJ.00.htm

INDEX